The World
in a Flash

How to Write Flash-Fiction

The World in... series, Vol. 1

Calum Kerr

GUMBO PRESS

Published by Gumbo Press

First Published 2014 by Gumbo Press.
Printed via CreateSpace.

Gumbo Press
18 Caxton Avenue
Bitterne
Southampton
SO19 5LJ
www.gumbopress.co.uk

A CIP Catalogue record for this book
is available from the British Library

ISBN 978-1497335738

Contents

For all the flash-fictioneers.

Introduction

In which we meet each other for the first time,
discuss the contents of this book,
and start to get a little bit excited.

Hello and welcome to this brief introduction to how to write flash-fiction.* While not claiming to be comprehensive, this book will look at the major aspects of writing very short stories, and show you how to get the best out of a limited word count.

---

*Throughout this book I will be writing the term as 'flash -fiction' with a hyphen as opposed to 'flash fiction' without. You will see it written both ways, but there is essentially no difference, just personal preference. There are also many other terms: 'sudden fiction', 'sudden prose', 'micro fiction', 'postcard fiction' 'short short stories' – which essentially refer to the same thing – and names for some of the individual types/lengths such as 'drabbles' (exactly 100 words), 'dribbles' (exactly 50 words) and the infamous 'six-word story'. For ease of understanding, this book will stick to talking about flash-fiction, but you should be able to apply most of the ideas to all the different types and lengths of prose writing.

The book is made up of chapters dealing with each of the main aspects in turn, discussing their features, and providing examples, and contains a number of exercises for you to complete to help you on your way.

It starts, as you might expect, by introducing the basic ideas and techniques and explaining just what this thing called 'flash-fiction' actually is. It then continues by looking at: the use of prompts, crafting characters, hooking your reader, developing plots, writing dialogue, picking a perspective and structuring your stories. It ends by examining methods for shaping, crafting and editing your stories, seeking publication, and a selection of sample flash-fictions to illustrate the ideas discussed.

As you go through each chapter there will be exercises to complete. Please look out for instructions such as '**DO IT NOW!**' which will appear when you should complete the exercise before you carry on reading, and '**TOOLBOX**' which indicates an exercise which is useful over and over again and which you should expect to do more than once.

If you go through this book in order, and follow the various instructions, you should develop a deeper understanding of flash-fictions, their many, many forms, and how to get the best out of them. However, there is no restriction on how you use this book, and picking and choosing from amongst the ideas and exercises will also give you good practise. And that is one of the key things about writing anything, and especially flash-fiction: practise makes perfect. So, when you have finished, do consider going back and trying the exercises again. Each time you attempt them, you will learn something new, and develop your skills.

This book is based on content I have used in my online courses, and in numerous writing workshops. It is based upon experience gained from over thirty years of writing, more than ten years of teaching Creative Writing, and from academic research into the field. After all of that crafting and honing, I hope you find it useful.

Finally, at the end, I have included some of my own flash-fictions as samples so you can see the various ideas in action.

But that's enough waffle, what say we get on?

1. What is flash-fiction?

*In which many different definitions are tried on —
in a manner Cinderella would have recognised —
until one is found to fit.*

Apologies to you if you feel you already know the answer to this, but a quick online search for an answer to this question will show you there are almost as many definitions of flash-fiction as there are writers working within the form, so it might be worth seeking a little clarity, at least in terms of the flash-fictions discussed in this book.

The first thing to remember is that a flash-fiction is a short, short story. So, as with other short stories it should feature one or more characters, some events, and some sense of a journey having been taken by the character. It also, because of its short nature, often features only part of a story and refers to a much larger story which occurs off the page.

Many definitions, for the purposes of magazines

and competitions looking for submissions, have to do with length. Some places say a flash is a story under 1000 words, some under 500, some 250, some 150, some 100, some 69 words exactly, etc. So, how do we choose? Well, for the purposes of this book let's assume we are talking about 500 words, somewhere nicely in the middle, long enough to allow some room to move, short enough to not be too scary.

I should say now, that if you look at the flash-fictions I have published, you will see that some of them exceed the upper-limit of 1000 words stated above. This would, by anybody's standards, make them fully-fledged short stories, rather than flashes. So what's going on there?

Well, I still feel able to call them 'flash-fictions' because for me there is more to flash-fiction than simply length. Length is a convenient way that publishers or competition judges can evaluate the form, and a handy way to include or exclude submissions, but it is essentially using the word 'flash' to define the speed of the *reader*'s experience. For the purposes of this book, I feel it is more useful to create a definition which applies to the *writer*'s experience instead. So, instead of something which can be *read* in a flash, we are talking about something which can be *written* in a flash.

To this end, when I write my flash-fictions, of whatever length, they happen in a particular way:

First, I write from a prompt. These prompts can be anything, quotes, pictures, music, over-hearings, news-stories, paint colour names, pretty much anything that can spark an idea in your mind. We will be looking more closely at these, and how to use them, in the next chapter.

Second, after a few moments of thinking time I start writing and do my best not to stop until it is done; writing it in a single sitting and with as few pauses for thought as I can.

So, in this definition, we are not concerned with length – certainly not in the first draft. It is, instead, a story written without any prior planning, from a prompt, and completed in a single 'flash' of writing. Sometimes it might be six words long, sometimes it's sixteen hundred, but the principle with which it was written is always the same.

As you can probably imagine, however, this kind of exercise lends itself to writing shorter short stories, so in general the pieces produced by this method fall around the 300-500 word mark. From this you can see that the 'flash' method of production meets up with the 'flash' limits set by publishers and judges.

However, there is more to our definition than this, and one thing we need to state is:

It's not a poem.

Flash-fictions are not just about the length of time it takes to write or read them, there is something more going on, something which will play a large part in our discussion of the form in this book.

There is another type of writing out there which is short, and written in prose, but which is not a flash-fiction. It's called a 'prose poem', and arguments often occur between writers and academics about the difference between the two. There is a difference, and it's important to realise it, but it's also important to know that flash-fictions do share at least some of their DNA with poetry.

The job of a poem is often to take a particular topic or theme and have a really good look at it, place it under a microscope, subject it to interrogation or comparison, and produce a new understanding of it. The job of a short story is to tell a story which may include revealing some new understanding or perspective, but that will emerge from transformation of the character, rather than simply through interrogation of the original idea.

So, in short, we might say that a story starts at A and moves to B, whereas a poem starts at A and has a really good look at it without feeling the need to move on.*

In both cases we might feel differently about A when we have read to the end, but in the first case we will also have been on some kind of journey within the story.

Why is this important? Well, because when starting out writing flash-fiction, it's very easy to find yourself producing a prose poem rather than a flash-fiction – I know I did! – and that is not a bad thing, prose poetry is a wonderful form, but now you will hopefully know it when you see it.

Flash-fiction does use language to its fullest though, like poetry.

Almost all words carry associations and connotations which expand our understanding of them beyond the simple dictionary definition. As such, we can use them in prose or poetry to create the most meaning in the shortest space

---

* I realise this is a wild generalisation which ignores narrative poetry and other poetic genres, but I hope any poets reading this will forgive the simplification.

by allowing those extra associations to tag along. So, when writing flash-fictions, you will, at times, find yourself thinking like a poet:

> …is 'cyan' better than 'blue'. It's more specific, sure, but is it a bit obscure. Would 'azure' be okay, or is that too fancy? If I use 'blue' maybe I can tie in something about music and then the melancholy of the blues might be there, yes, okay, I'll stick with 'blue' but I'll send my character into 'twelve bars' later on…

This is perfectly natural and normal and does not mean that you are writing prose poetry, it means that you're getting the hang of writing flash-fiction, a form in which you need to ask a lot of the words you choose, and assume that your reader will do the work necessary to 'get it' because you don't have the time to tell them everything.

So, after all that, just what is flash-fiction?

Flash-fiction is a short story, almost always under 1000 words, and most often under 500 words. It uses those words, by straight-forward story-telling and by association and connotation, to tell a snapshot of a story and, at the same time, to imply a much larger tale. It comes in many different forms, can be written in many different styles, and can exist within any genre or genres. It is a bite-sized piece of fiction which leaves the reader to fill in many of the blanks and, as a result, provides them with a satisfying reading experience, despite the short length.

All of which is fine, but flash-fiction is also something which is personal to the writer. I have taken care in this overview to give my own personal definition of the form within which I work, but if you talk to other flash-fiction writers, you may get slightly different definitions, or emphases on different aspects. This does not mean that they're wrong, or that I am, just that flash-fiction is still an evolving form, and because of its length, is often a site of experimentation.

For most purposes, however, and for the purposes of this book, the definition above should be enough, and it will certainly give you an understanding of what you are doing as you start to forge your own definition.

EXERCISE

We haven't covered any of the individual features of flash-fiction yet, but that doesn't matter, it's time for you to do some writing.

DO IT NOW! and TOOLBOX

[This is a very useful exercise which requires no specific preparation. As well as asking you to undertake this exercise before you carry on with the rest of the book, it has been labelled as a **TOOLBOX** exercise as this is a useful way calm to your mind in preparation for writing, to form ideas for stories, and to force yourself to put pen to paper when writer's block is threatening. As such, you should return to this exercise regularly.]

Find a watch, clock, sand-timer or stopwatch which will allow you to measure exactly one minute at a time. Don't worry, I'll wait…

Got it? Good.

Now, have it somewhere you can see it clearly and then fetch a pen and a piece of paper. This is an exercise to be done by hand, rather than keyboard.

Now, get yourself settled and comfortable and get ready to go. You are going to time yourself for **just one minute** and in that minute you are going to write about **what you can see**. This could be on the table in front of you, in the room around you, what you can see out of the window, anything. How you choose to interpret the instruction is up to you. But try to be as full and descriptive as you can. Are there metaphors or similes you can use? If so, chuck them in. Colours? Good. Emotions? Excellent.

Okay, know what you have to do? Then… Go!

…

Well, that was a quick minute, wasn't it?

Reset your clock, get yourself ready because we're going to go again, but this time it's **one minute on what you can hear**. Inside or outside, loud or faint, or nothing more than your pulse in your ears.

Ready… Go!

…

Back already? Well done! Okay, I think you're getting the hang of this. So, reset the clock and this time it's **one minute on what you can feel**. Under your hands, your feet, your bottom on that chair…

Ready … Go!

…

You're smiling. I can see you've guessed the next one already. So, **one minute on what you can smell**.

Ready … Go!

…

Nearly there. Ready for **one last minute on what you can taste**? Good!

Ready … Go!

…

And relax!

There, that wasn't so bad, was it?

Now take the time to tinker with what you have written, tidy it up until you are happy with it. Don't worry if you haven't written anything resembling a story, that's not what this exercise is about. This is an exercise which brings you to yourself, cuts out the world, and reminds you that you are a living breathing creature with five active senses.

This is a great **TOOLBOX** exercise in that you can do it in many different places and never have the same input twice, producing a wide range of different work. But also, when you are trying to write and finding it difficult, it gives you something to write, calms the mind, and brings you back to the basics.

Consider doing this exercise again in different places. Take a pad and pen with you wherever you go (as any writer should) and whenever you have a spare five minutes, do it again. You will be surprised by what emerges in different places and different states of mind.

2. Prompts

*In which we scour the world
for inspiration and find it
lurking everywhere.*

Okay, now we've got you writing something, let's think about starting to write flash-fictions.

I previously mentioned the concept of 'prompts', but what exactly are they and how do they work?

A prompt is anything which triggers a response in you that can lead to a story. However, this is not about something creating that wonderful thing 'inspiration', but finding something useful that will allow you to start writing.

Inspiration, as much as it can be understood, occurs when one or more things catch the mind's attention and turn them into story. I say 'the mind' rather than 'your' because oftentimes this attention catching occurs on a sub-conscious level, and only becomes conscious as an idea develops. The mind captures these things and bombards them with questions: who? what? where? when? how? why? and the writer's classic: what if? As it starts to answer these questions, story ideas start to form, characters and plots come into being, and eventually, as it grows larger and bobs up on the surface of the mind, it becomes that amazing thing we call 'inspiration'.

As any writer knows, this is a wonderful moment. However, many fruitless and frustrating hours can be spent waiting for this to happen by itself. Using prompts is a way of forcing the issue, and doing all of the work out in the open without waiting for the machines of the subconscious to spit out their products.

So, what do prompts look like?

Prompts are pictures, words, phrases, objects, overheard conversations, pieces of music or anything which you can use to inspire you to write something. Writers who use prompts gather these things as they go through their daily lives and store them up, either in their physical form: postcards, objects, photographs, etc. or by writing them down in a notebook.

DO IT NOW! and **TOOLBOX**

This is not so much an exercise as it is a general and ongoing instruction:

Get yourself a notebook!

Make sure it is small enough to fit in your pocket, or bag; small enough that you can always carry it with you. Add a pen or pencil to it, too. Now, carry this with you at all times, so you can note down things which interest you, things you see, things you hear, things you think of. You never know when one of these things will provide the useful basis for a story.

Maybe you want to browse a bookshop and write down some titles of books you've never read. Maybe you prefer music so want to spend an hour in HMV doing the same with album or song titles. Perhaps you overhear people talking in the street and their words sound useful. Maybe it's road signs, or the way the houses on your street look, or a collection of postcards, or really, anything at all.*

---

*I once wrote down an idea in a notebook and it was 8 years later before I finally turned it into a story.

DO IT NOW!

Words themselves are useful prompts. If you search the internet, you will find many 'word lists' and these are often useful sources of inspiration. The following is a list of words such as you might gather for prompts.

Look at each of the words in turn and then, on a piece of paper, write down the ideas, images, thoughts, etc that come to you when you see each word. Don't try and over-think it, if you run out of ideas, move on to the next. You can go through them again when you have finished, but you should try and record your first reactions rather than perform an intense study. Oh, and don't Google them, this is about your personal response, not your research. And, again, this is about generating quick replies to the words, not about writing full stories.

- Purple
- City
- Impulse
- Girl
- South
- Bewilderment
- Obsession
- Play
- Prison

- Lazy
- Open
- Friend

Okay, done that?

Now I'd like you to think about which prompt or prompts were the most useful to you in terms of the number of ideas generated. Why were they useful? Did any of them suggest a story? More than one story? Does this fit in with the kind of things you write or read?

There is no right answer to this, it's about what works for you.

How to turn Prompts into Stories

Okay, so now you have a bunch of images and ideas, but how do we turn these into stories?

Well, let me start by giving you my own list of associations for a word not in the list: *Work*.

Work – boredom, stress, something to be got through, offices, suits, coffee machines, water coolers, the whizz of printers and photocopiers, filing, nylon carpets, bosses, inter-office romances, play, something fulfilling, a great job, the thing you want to do, dream job, toil, sweat, hard labour, prison, strange jobs, steeplejack, Forth Bridge painter, rest

As you look through that, you can almost chart what my brain was doing. It started with the obvious, concepts, then went into some sensory input – sights and sounds and possibly taste and smell (coffee) – it then started to branch out into larger ideas which feel like story (romance) before flipping the idea and looking at its opposites or by uncommon associations with the concept.

One of the wonders of language is that many words are defined by what they are not, and as such they carry their opposites with them by association (these pairs, such as up/down, day/night or left/right are termed *Binary Oppositions*). Work is one of these. So it's hard to think of the concept of work without the ideas of 'play' or 'rest' coming into it. Years of *Mars* adverts haven't helped either.

So, how can we turn this list of ideas into a story?

Well, it is often said that story comes from conflict. That doesn't mean that every story has to be about war, it can be as simple as trying to decide between the croissant and the Danish, but without conflict there is no progression, no drama, no story.

Where do we find conflict in the idea of work? It comes in the gaps between these oppositions; in the gaps between 'something to be got through' and 'dream job' between 'boredom' and 'stress' and 'inter-office romances' and between 'work' and 'play'.

So, I can immediately think of a number of stories that might emerge from this list:

- Someone who's bored in their job, lands their dream job, and finds it just as tedious.

- Someone for whom work becomes something they want to get to as soon as they can because they've fallen in love with the tea lady.

- Someone who is going through the mill of their daily grind but whose mind is always on the things they are going to do when work finishes

- And on, and on.

But what is the key word in all of those ideas? 'Someone'. In order to turn any of those ideas or images into a story, we need to have a 'character' for them to happen to. Story without character is just plot. And, to be frank, plot on its own is boring. In the next chapter, we'll move on to talk about characters and how we can get them walking and talking.

EXERCISES

One good area for prompts can be song titles. They are often abstract enough to inspire whilst being concrete enough to give direction.

Let's take the song from the '80s, 'Ghost Town' by *The Specials* (don't worry if you don't know the song, that really doesn't matter. In fact, it's maybe easier if you don't know it). What images do those two words conjure in your mind?

Here's some of mine:

Ghost – haunting, haunted house, the dead, the living dead, zombies, vampires, horror, sadness, lost, found, memories...

Town – city, urban, crime, cars, shops, busy, people, uptown, downtown, lights, music, litter...

Ghost Town – a Specials song, deserted streets, emptiness, the 80s, unemployment, desolation and desperation...

Now, from all of those thoughts, some on their own, and some in combination, it should be possible to write a story.

Use the song above, or chose a song title of your own, and explore your own associations, then write down a possible story idea. It doesn't need to be a whole story, just the idea of one, a few sentence outline. Try to do it in under 5 minutes.

When you have done that, have a go at actually writing your story, and consider the following things as you do so. Who is your character? Where and when is it set? What's the main event in the story? Is there a theme?

These are all topics we will cover in the following chapters, so don't worry too much about them, but they are all keys which open a story up, so worth bearing in mind. And don't worry about quality, this is about producing something from a prompt, whatever it might be.

3. Characters

In which we invent a host of people, make them walk and talk, give them hopes and desires, and then sit them down for a chat.

Characters are the driving force of a story. But – I hear you ask – surely that's plot? Well, if you go for plot without character, we either end up with a synopsis, or we end up with bad writing. I'm not going to mention any names here, but I'm sure you can think of some authors who prize plot above character and their writing suffers for it.*

So, maybe I should have said that characters are the driving force of a *good* story. And if we think about it, this makes sense as story should

---

*I freely confess to having made this mistake myself. In my *flash365* project I wrote a story called 'Vision On' about a world which descends into madness because people could watch TV through contact lenses. It's a nice idea, but it's not a story, it's the synopsis of a novel. What makes it not a story? No characters...

come from all those things which drive us as human beings – the need to survive, find food, find warmth and shelter, find love and companionship, and to find happiness. There are more, but most of them boil down to these. This might mean a story in which your character is stranded on a desert island trying to find enough food to avoid starvation. It might mean your character is in a tea-shop trying to choose which kind of cake they want, but it comes down to the same needs expressed through character.

So, the way that we turn our images/ideas/concepts from the prompts exercise into a story, is by introducing character.

Character is always the thing that we fall in love with in a story. People love *Star Wars*, and this might be because of the way that Han Solo shoots the alien in the bar, or the way Luke shoots the exhaust vent at the end. But they love these events because of the characters who do them. If it was just any old person doing these, no-one would care. Likewise people love the Harry Potter books, but not because of the action and the spells, but because of the people involved in these things.

Now you might think that it's hard to create well-rounded, fully-fledged characters in something as short as a flash-fiction. And it is, but not as hard as you would think. There seems to be two reasons for this. One is that we make snap judgements about people, so how you introduce a character will tell a reader a lot about them. The other is that stereotypes are wonderful things.

Yes, you heard me right. I'm advocating stereotypes. *But how can you possibly say that?* I hear you cry. Well, we don't have space to flesh out a full character, so we can use one from the cupboard, and then lay individuality on top. This allows us to start from a base level of character and then add detail.

So, think for a moment about a character who is a twenty-one years old, middle-class, white male.

Okay, got him in your head?

- Is he a student in his final year at University?
- Is he a waster who still lives with his mum?
- Is he a go-getter working his way up in his company?
- Has he just moved into his first flat with his girlfriend?
- None of these?

It doesn't matter who he is, he will probably fit into one category or another which we could term a stereotype. What this allows us to do is to cover the basics quickly and then lay out details on top.

So, how would we convey these basics?

Names

Names are very important in stories. All of our men are white and middle class, so they will have a type of name chosen from that particular sector. Other classes and other races would have different names. Names also convey age. Think of what you can infer about a character called 'Albert' versus one called 'Dean'. Many writers I know have bookmarks on 'Baby Names' websites. These can provide useful inspiration, and often have 'Favourite' lists of names going back many years, which allow for period settings.

Occupations /Activities

We spend so many hours of our lives in work that what we do there informs a large part of our personalities. We also assume a lot about a character based on their occupation. Are they an architect or a bricklayer, a teacher or an accountant, an office clerk, a writer, or unemployed? Likewise, the activities and hobbies that we chose to do outside of work are equally important. What someone does for fun tells us a lot about them.

Friends and Family

To paraphrase Philip Larkin, our personalities are formed and developed by our interactions with our family. So, who they are, whether they are alive or dead, and how they interact with a character can be a useful way of giving information. And, just as activities are useful to contrast against work, so a character's friends – the people they chose to spend time with – can give you a lot of insight.

Mannerisms

It's worth also thinking about the ticks and habits that your character has. These can be small details which give a large amount of character information, even if it's just the difference between someone who has to have their DVD collection in alphabetical order, versus someone who never puts an empty crisp packet in the bin if there is a spare patch of floor on which to leave it.

How to move from Type to Character

How we decide to combine or diverge from these basic ideas can then lead us to our individual character.

For example: if Percival Bently-Smythe is dressed in a rock t-shirt and found in a crack-den, that tells us a huge amount of story. Likewise if Chantelle Smith is wearing an Armani suit and closing a million pound deal, that does the same thing.

DO IT NOW! and TOOLBOX

Write brief character descriptions for four characters from various backgrounds. Think about including at least the following details:

Name
Age
Place of birth
Ethnicity
Class
Marital status
Sexual orientation
Occupation
Leisure activities

These will give you your baseline. They allow you to pluck a character from the cupboard and customise them. Notice that I haven't included physical descriptions. These are rarely useful in terms of fleshing out a character unless the story is to be about their broken spectacles, dyeing their hair, fixing their teeth, etc. And in that case they are character specific.

Now we can add details which will break us away from our stereotypes and into real characters:

Do they have a secret?
How do they feel about their family?
How do they feel about their work?
How do they feel about themselves?
What do they do when they get bad news?
How do they celebrate when they get good news?
What is their favourite memory?
What keeps them awake at night?

Etc.

With this second list, we are starting to add those details which make this person different from everyone else, and take us away from the baseline of stereotype. I have added the 'etc.' because the list here is pretty much endless.

Think of your own questions and add the answers.

What you have done is create rounded characters with rich internal lives.

Characters in a Flash

Now, if you were writing a novel, this would give you the details which could emerge over the course of 100,000 words. But in a flash how do you fit all of that in?

The simple answer is, you don't. One or two is all you will have space for, but one or two is enough:

- A twenty-one year old university student doing his finals who lies awake worrying about bowel cancer.

- A male twenty-one year old go-getter who is secretly in love with his male boss, even though he's always been straight.

- A forty year old woman with three children and a workaholic husband who dreams of becoming a ballroom dancer.

The extra details take our stereotypes and turn them into a character. They also, I hope you notice, suggest the start of a story.

Now, the process you have gone through above is a great one of generating character-based prompts in and of itself, but it is also – in a smaller way – the process that you go through when moving from an idea-based prompt to a story. You need to think, 'Who is this happening to?' and 'What makes them important/different/ interesting?'

EXERCISE

Take one of your selection of prompts/ideas/ concepts generated in the last chapter, and turn it into a story. In the process, think about where the drama/conflict/story is coming from. And spend some time thinking about who the character is who is involved in the story, what makes them different/interesting/important, put it all together, and write their story.

When you have finished, write down your thought processes on this series of activities. Reflecting on what you have written, why you have written it the way you have, and what you have learned from it is the best way to build your skills and confidence as a writer.

4. Hooks and Questions

*In which we grab the reader's
attention, sink our claws in,
and refuse to let go.*

If you are a reader, and have friends who are also readers, chances are you have had a conversation about your favourite opening lines. Whether your favourite was "Call me Ishamel." from Herman Melville's *Moby Dick*, "It was the day my grandmother exploded." the opening of Iain Banks's *The Crow Road*, or something else altogether, chances are there is an opening sentence which has lodged in your mind.

There is a reason for this. These sentences have been crafted to grab your attention and make you want to carry on with the story.

That's what a good beginning does. It forces you to read the next sentence because you want answers to the questions posed in the first. If it's a good second sentence, it simply asks more questions, as does the third, and

41

before you know it: you're hooked.

The literary theorist, Roland Barthes, was a 'structuralist' who spent some time categorising the different types of sentences and phrases we find in fiction (particularly in *S/Z*, Roland Barthes, Blackwell, 2002). He discovered five separate types, which he called 'codes'. One was presenting actions, two referred to people and things, one referred to common knowledge, and one was posing questions. He called this last type the 'hermeneutic code'. And the purpose of this code was not simply to construct phrases which pose questions to the reader, but to pose questions that can only be answered from within the text. Thus, when we read an opening sentence like those above, we immediately want to know who the narrator is, who they are speaking about, what's going on and why.

The hermeneutic code is absolutely crucial to flash-fiction. At the beginning of this book, in trying to define what flash-fiction actually is, I talked about the way it uses language and the way it tells a story by implication and connotation. This can occur because of the use of the hermeneutic code. By writing sentences which pose questions and ask the reader to do some work, often for the entirety of a story (bar the ending, usually, but more on that later) you are asking them to find answers which only exist within the story, but which are often not provided, only hinted at, or described by an absence.

This, I believe, is what makes the best flash-fictions work. They hook the reader, they pull them along on a line of questions, and the reader needs to decode the language, the setting, their knowledge of stories, and the few 'clues' in the story, in order to discover what has happened and what it all means. And for those reasons, it leads to a very engaging, immersive and memorable story.

Of course, in a story like that, the ending is going to be crucial. In many cases, it's the one place where the questions stop, and some answers are provided. This, I believe, is what has led to the definition of flash-fiction which compares it to a joke: a feed and then a punch-line; and to comments about 'twists in the tale'.

A good flash is not simply a joke, and a twist in the tale which is nothing more than a random event, a *deus ex machina*, satisfies no-one. No, the ending of a flash-fiction should be the moment of clarification, the point at which the tangled snarl of questions is pulled taut and the straight line from opening to ending is finally seen.

Now, this is not the only way to write a flash, but some structural analysis of flash-fictions shows that many are written in this way, making good use of the possibilities of the hermeneutic code, then resolving the questions at the end. There is something eminently satisfying about it. It's not a model for writing flash, but it's fascinating to see it in action.

As such, when writing flash, it is good to practise hooking the reader with your questions, and pulling them through your story in hope of an answer.

DO IT NOW!

Without looking them up, see if you can identify the following opening lines. If you can't, try to work out when they might have been written, and the genre of the book etc. Also, decide for yourself whether these work as 'hooks' to get you into the story quickly. Would you want to read on, or are you bored?

'It is a truth universally acknowledged, that a single man in possession of a good fortune, must be in want of a wife.'

'It was a bright cold day in April, and the clocks were striking thirteen.'

'It was the best of times, it was the worst of times, it was the age of wisdom, it was the age of foolishness, it was the epoch of belief, it was the epoch of incredulity, it was the season of Light, it was the season of Darkness, it was the spring of hope, it was the winter of despair.'

'If you really want to hear about it, the first thing you'll probably want to know is where I was born, and what my lousy childhood was like, and how my parents were occupied and all before they had me, and all that David Copperfield kind of crap, but I don't feel like going into it, if you want to know the truth.'

'It was a pleasure to burn.'

'TRUE! nervous, very, very dreadfully nervous I had been and am; but why WILL you say that I am mad?'

'_____, who was usually very late in the mornings, save upon those not infrequent occasions when he was up all night, was seated at the breakfast table.'

'Behavioral Science, the FBI section that deals with serial murder, is on the bottom floor of the Academy building at

Quantico, half-buried in the earth.'

'There was no possibility of taking a walk that day.'

'The sky above the port was the color of television, tuned to a dead channel.'

'I had been making the rounds of the Sacrifice Poles the day we heard my brother had escaped.'

Okay? Got some answers and some guesses? Now, before you move on, really do give some thought about which ones appeal to you and why? What are they doing that intrigues you or turns you off?

Having done that you can now feel free to look up the answers (available in the Appendix). If you didn't know them were you right about the date and genre? Did any surprise you?

Next job is to go to your bookshelves and take down some of your favourite (prose) books. Have a look at the opening lines. Are they good hooks? Do they grab you and make you want to read on? Or are they let-downs? Consider why.

It would probably be possible to devote a whole book purely to writing the first sentences of stories, but here are some thoughts.

I. Good hooks ask questions

Those opening sentences which grab our attention and make us want to read on are giving us only a small amount of information. Just enough for us to go who? what? but...? how...? Huh? They make us want to read on because we need the answers to those questions. The best ones are giving us something integral to the story which will be answered by the story as it unfolds.

The weaker ones are the ones that make us go 'Yep', 'Fair enough', 'Enough said' or similar. They are closed and finished statements in and of themselves, and lead nowhere.

It is quite hard to write a completely closed opening line, but the more intriguing the opening, the more questions it poses, the more we want to read on. Strangeness, obscurity or character names work well here because they also give us a flavour of what is to come, and we are already buying into the plot or character before we have even really begun.

2.   Write them last

Especially if you are writing in a 'flash' from a prompt, then it is unlikely that the first draft of your first sentence will encapsulate the glory of your whole story. So, when starting off, don't worry too much about the opening sentence. In the first draft it is just a way to get going. But then, when you have finished, you can go back and edit/change/delete/add and craft something which leaves your reader hanging from your hook.

3.   Incorporate them into the plot

The weaker hooks for me are the ones which make general statements, provide background or, worst of all, describe the weather. The ones which work best for me are the ones which dive straight in.

There is a principal in story writing called 'Chekov's Gun'. This states that if a significant item such as a gun is introduced into the story at the beginning it *must* be fired by the end. A gun, because of what it signifies, can never just be set dressing. Likewise, to avoid a *deus ex machina* where the ending is a complete surprise to the reader and suggests the author has been sneaky (or lazy), if you want a gun to be fired at the end, it needs to mentioned earlier. So, if your ending has an object or concept in it that the whole plot hangs on, you need to ensure it's up there at the top. Why not have it in the opening sentence?

So, having given some deep thought to hooks, here is an exercise for you:

TOOLBOX

Write ten opening lines which will 'hook' and intrigue your readers. Try to vary how they work, think about incorporating concepts, names, objects etc. And think about working in different genres. Do they work differently depending on genre?

This is a good Toolbox exercise because it involves concentrating just on the one sentence and what it is doing. As I mentioned above, it frees you from having to write the whole story, but it can be a good way to get started if you're stuck, and a good way of getting something down on the page.

It is also useful in two more ways:

1. The practise of writing single sentences which produce questions helps you with creating them over and over throughout a flash.

---

2. Coming up with an idea for a single opening sentence is relatively straight-forward, but who says you have to stop there? You could write the rest of the story!

5. Plots

*In which many things happen,
in a variety of orders, and we turn
some of them into stories.*

The plots which appear in flash-fictions are little different to those used in short stories, novels, plays, TV or films. They still focus on the basic human desires, needs and anxieties – life, death, love, hate, sex, violence, wealth, poverty – and any combination thereof. The difference between flash-fiction and those other forms is that, in a flash-fiction, you have very little space in which to develop a plot, so you must include just a suggestion of the larger idea, and provide the rest by implication. Readers have a good understanding of plot, so a little information can go a long way.

Before we can look at how to use plot in a flash-fiction, it's important to understand just what we are talking about when we use the terms 'plot' and 'story'.

Simply put, 'plot' describes the events which occur. This is the sum total of the events you will be using, in chronological order.

So, if someone asks you the plot of a movie you can probably tell it quite quickly:

Star Wars: Evil Empire vs plucky Rebels. Farm-boy Luke buys some droids which lead him to leave his planet, join the rebellion and blow up a big-old space station.

Four Weddings and a Funeral: English fop falls in love with an American woman over the course of four weddings (and a funeral) and finally gets it into his head that she is the one for him. He stops messing around and the two of them end up together but, ironically, not married.

The Remains of the Day: A butler serves in the same house for decades, under different employers, and witnesses the changes in British society before and after the Second World War.

But while these tell us the essential details, they lack the punch of the films/novel in question. So what happens to change them from a list of events into something special? Story happens, that's what.

As an academic I have spent quite a bit of time looking at the differences between plot and story. Plot is, as detailed above, all of the events laid out in chronological order. Story is the way that those events are selected and related *in this instance* with the addition of character, theme, emotion, etc.* The italics on 'in this instance' are worth noticing because 'story' refers to the particular version of your plot that you have chosen to tell.

It's also important to think about plot as the underlying events which we customise for each story because, as you have possibly heard, there are supposedly only seven plots in the whole world. **

---

* See Chapter 7, on *Perspective and Structure,* for more on how to individualise your story.

** There are many arguments for and against this, by the way, and I have a separate argument that there is maybe only one plot. You might want to read Christopher Booker's *The Seven Basic Plots* and Joseph Campbell's *The Hero With A Thousand Faces*, and see what you think.

So how, I hear you ask, if there are only seven plots, do we have so very many films and stories? That's because every time we come to one of those plots we add our own details and tell it in our own way. This retelling of an existent plot with its own particular details is 'story'.

One example is the basic romantic comedy plot:

- Two people meet
- they start to fall in love
- something happens to drive them apart
- this something is overcome
- they come together again at the end and get married (either literally or symbolically).

This basic plot fits *Much Ado about Nothing*, it fits *The Sound of Music*, and it fits *Shrek*. It also fits millions of other stories, in millions of per-mutations, and we never seem to get tired of it.

The same is true with the other plots. The plot known as 'The Quest', for instance, is *The Odyssey*, *On The Road* and *Lord of the Rings*.

What makes these different is the details overlaid on top of the plot to make it into an individual story. It is also to do with the order in which the events are told, and the structure of the story itself. There will be more on structure in Chapter 7.

Now, I'm sure you can find ways to circumvent these plots and do different things – but the reason these plots have been identified is that they are the plots that readers and viewers seem to find the most satisfying. When we write or read a story which we think works well, chances are that the underlying events fit with one of those plots.

EXERCISE

Overleaf are the outlines of the seven basic plots as described by Christopher Brooker.* Use one of these to write a flash-fiction. Remember that you should be trying to keep your story under 500 words, so you are probably going to have to open at the end of the story and either feed in the details of what has gone before, or imply them. You are going to need to create character and narrative voice, and all those details which

Christopher Booker, *The Seven Basic Plots: Why We Tell Stories*. (London: Continuum, 2005)

make this oft-written plot your own particular piece of work.

My advice is to start with writing out the events of the whole story – construct a plot from a collection of short sentences which lay out what happens, decide on character and theme etc – and then decide which part(s) need to told.

The 7 Basic Plots

Overcoming the Monster – the protagonist, or his society, are faced by a great evil which our hero(ine) must seek out and defeat.

Rags to Riches – the protagonist starts off in a low station in life which they improve over the course of the story, emerging with wealth which is still tempered with benevolence and wisdom.

The Quest – there is something out there which our protagonist needs, so they set off to find it.

Voyage and Return – the protagonist sets off on a journey in which they have many adventures before finally returning home.

Comedy – Two protagonists are destined to be

together, something prevents this, and then it is overcome. Traditionally ends with a marriage and many subplots being revealed and reconciled.

Tragedy – The protagonist is a villain, usually in a position of power. The story sees their decline and fall and their eventual death is a cause for celebration.

Rebirth – The protagonist is a villain, usually in a position of power. The story sees their decline and fall, but with this decline comes wisdom and they are able to redeem themselves to become a better person.

6. Dialogue

*In which we talk about talking,
chat about chatting,
and yak about yakking.*

As a writer of flash-fiction, dialogue can be one of your best tools for getting information across quickly. It can tell us a lot about character, it can inform us about plot and setting, and it is a really good way of moving a story along.

Plus, readers like dialogue. I have had many conversations with people who say if they are faced with a page of unbroken description (especially a single paragraph which fills the page) then their heart sinks and they flick forward to see where the next piece of dialogue comes in.

Dialogue is very often short and quick to read, and it makes the reader move more quickly through the story. So, if you want the reader to speed up and get excited, dialogue can be a real help.

Before we go deeper, let's start with an exercise.

DO IT NOW!

This one may take you some time, but it's worth doing before you move on.

You need to find a way to listen to people and the way they talk. Scan through the TV and radio and find some people who are talking without scripts – people being interviewed or calling in to a talk show etc. are usually the best.

What I want you to do is *really* listen. This is not about understanding what is being said, but the actual words and sounds. Disconnect from understanding and hear everything.

Okay... off you go.

...

Back? Good.

Now hopefully you noticed some or all of the following things:

- People don't talk in complete sentences. We tend to stop and start, change tack and tense and topic mid-thought, and often just tail off in the middle of a...

- People pronounce words and use grammar differently depending on where they are from in the country/world.

- Young people and old people talk differently, as do people of different classes, different education levels, and from different professional backgrounds.

- People have verbal ticks and words that they, you know, use without even realising it.

- People often say pointless things – filler.

- People rarely give speeches. Conversation is a ping-pong game, not golf.

Some of these are useful when we write dialogue, some not so much, but let's look at them in turn:

Complete sentences
This is worth noting because if you want your dialogue to be realistic, then you need to find a way to avoid the complete, perfectly gram-matical sentence.

"In dialogue you can fragment. Split up. Use just phrases. Words. Tail off... lose your train of... you know... thingy... Change topic half way through a – oh, I just saw a squirrel!!"

Pronunciation
Altering spelling to reflect pronunciation can be an effective way of representing accent and dialect. I shall deal more with this below as it is a thorny topic.

Differences
Without changing spelling, you can still give a lot of information about the speaker by their vocabulary, the length of their sentences and their grammar.

Verbal Ticks
"Tying in with the previous point, adding, you know, those little verbal ticks, like, that everyone, kind of, you know, sort of uses, all of the, you know, time, kind of thing, can really show something about, like, character, and that."

Filler
"Nice day isn't it. How are you? Keeping well? I think it might rain later. Oh well, I might go for a walk if I can be bothered. Then again, it might stay fine. I like nice weather."

Annoying in real life, but can tell you a lot about character or mood.

Speeches
"The one thing you will never find, when you listen to the conversation of the ordinary man in the street, is that they will never, never, make declarative speeches to each other – of any sort – about the things which are going on. This makes a single speech not as useful for explaining the intricacies of your plot as the writers of many mainstream television series, and Hollywood blockbusters, would have us believe. No. It is just not the way. So if you want to get information across, you need to find a way to make it into conversation."

"By asking questions?"

"Yes, that is one good way."

"Or by having other people with bits of the information?"

"I think my colleague should take that one…"

All of which is great, but where does it leave us with the wonderful world of dialogue?

Well, dialogue is where your characters get to speak. And we want to hear their voices. It is the ultimate in showing, not telling, as we actually get to hear the words that come out of the character's mouth. So, you need to do two things. You need to make them individual, and you need to make them count.

Making them individual

If there are two characters, it's not so bad. We start with one character, the next one to talk is the other one, and we go back and forth. So far, so good. But have you ever read a book where you weren't sure who was talking? Even when there were only two of them? That's because there was not enough difference between the two. You couldn't tell them apart. Once you get to three speakers or more, it gets even worse.

So, how do you solve this? Well, this is where all those little nuances come in. You don't need to do anything big and obvious, but listen to the character in your head, hear how they talk. Do they use any particular words? Do they say 'It is' rather than 'It's' and 'do not' rather than 'don't'? What is going to make them just a little different from your other characters and also tell us something about them at the same time?

Making them count

This is about writing dialogue that does something, rather than just to show character, or to fill the page. Earlier on I said that sometimes people say nothing when they talk.

And this is true. But your character should only be saying nothing if it serves the story. Otherwise, they should *really* say nothing.

So, if your character is a scatter-brain, you can show this in how they talk. If they are nervous because they're about to ask out that girl they really fancy, then talking about everything else but the topic is natural. However, if they run into a burning building, they should never stop to comment on the wallpaper.

TOOLBOX

I am going to give you permission now to do something that we (probably) all do anyway. I want you to eavesdrop.

You might choose the people you live with, or you might want to go out to a café, or you might leave it and do it at work. But I want you to listen in on some conversations and write down, as accurately as you can, what is actually said. Include all 'ticks', the 'ums' and 'ers', the digressions, tailings off, random turnings. Get as much as you can down.

Don't think about it while you are doing it. This is an exercise in listening and transcription.

Then when you have your over-hearings, take them somewhere else and have a look at them. Did you hear any interesting word-choices being made? Any verbal ticks? How did what you hear give you an insight into character.

This is a 'toolbox' exercise because there is nothing better than listening to people to pick up on real rhythms of speech, but as mentioned in the chapter on 'Prompts', eavesdropping is also a good way to get ideas for stories. A half-heard sentence can be an intriguing hook by itself.

Dialect

Okay, this is, as I said, a thorny topic. Dialect and accent are part of speech, we can't get away from them, but representing them on the page can be difficult.

A colleague of mine tells a story about a science-fiction book he once read. In this book an Englishman, an Irishman, a Scotsman and a Welshman all go up into space. (No, this is not a joke.) And whenever they talk, they do so in completely grammatical sentences (full sentences which sometimes turn into speeches... it really is very bad). And to differentiate between them, the Englishman always says 'old boy' at the end of his speeches. The Irishman finishes his with 'to be sure, begorrah.' The Scotsman always signs off with 'och aye the noo', and the Welshman with 'look you, boyo'. It is very, very bad. Please don't ever do this kind of thing unless you are being funny.*

However, you can't always go the opposite way and write everything phonetically in an Irvine Welsh *Trainspotting* style.

So, how do you show where someone is from? Well, telling us is a good start. If we know that a character comes from Kilmarnock, or Birmingham (UK or Alabama) or Delhi, then that tells us what kind of accent to imagine their speech in.

Beyond that, word choice can be important. Read around, listen to some voices from that place, are there regional words you can use? Do they order their words in a different way? Is there a way you can use normal spellings, but change the choice and order of words to give a slight flavour which will enhance what you have already told us?

Of course, you can go down the full dialect

---

*And even then, please don't do this.

route but my advice would be to do it only with accents/dialects that you know well, or that you have researched.

If you do want to do this, or somewhere in between, then you need to think about using phonetic spellings. Try not to use too many apostrophes to show missing letters as it becomes cluttered (if you want to know what I mean, have a look at Joseph's speeches in *Wuthering Heights*) but treat them as if these are the ways that the words are spelt in that dialect. It makes it easier on the reader.

Incorporation

The last thing to note about dialogue, and to some extent this is me un-teaching things you might have learned at school, is that speech needs minimal incorporation into the text around it.

Speech should do its own job and shouldn't need too much explication.

So, try to avoid using verbs other than 'said', 'asked' or 'replied', unless you absolutely have to. (So no 'he questioned' 'she averred', 'Billy vociferated'.)

Also, for the same reason, avoid adverbs (so no

'he said angrily', 'she asked enquiringly', 'Billy responded inspiringly').

These are signs that your speech is not doing enough work. If your person is angry, they need angry words. If they are in despair, they need despairing words. Don't just give them plain speech and hope that you can explain it in the outside text. Dialogue can do a lot of your work for you, so let it.

'Get out,' he said angrily.

is never going to be as good as

'If I ever see you in this house again, I swear to God I don't know what I shall do!'

Oh, and as for exclamation marks, they are just for exclamations. So, if someone is actually shouting, then you should use them. If they are just being funny or ironic, then don't.

EXERCISE

For this exercise you need to write a piece of dialogue. Sounds simple, doesn't it?

You should use only two characters, and I forbid you from using any other text at all. Tell a story purely through the conversation of the two characters. Give some sense of who they are, what their relationship is, what the story is and how it progresses, and bear in mind all of the various dos and don'ts expressed above.

If it helps you, why not start with one of your overheard conversations and see where it takes you? Or, use something from the prompts you have gathered.

If you are unsure, there is a sample story at the end of this book which might give you an idea of how this can work.

7. Perspective, Tense and Structure

In which you, me, him and her move backwards and forwards in time, swap, fragment and experiment.

Over the previous chapters we have looked at some of the various parts that make up flash-fictions – opening lines, characters, plots and dialogue. Now it is time to look not at *what* we tell in our stories, but *how* we tell them. We need to look at our storytellers, the ways in which they tell the story to us, and how they structure their tales.

Perspective

It takes a little effort to wrap your mind around it, but there are more people involved in the flash-fiction than just you, the author, and the reader who eventually enjoys it. There are two more people – imagined people – who we need to consider: 'The Narrator' and 'The Implied Reader'.

The Narrator

This is the voice that the author invents in order to tell the story. It comes in a variety of flavours:

First person: this is where the invented narrator is a character who takes part in the story. They tell the story from their own perspective as though the events of the plot had actually happened to them. They know their own actions, thoughts and feelings, but nothing of other characters except what comes through their senses. They use the personal pronouns: 'I', 'me' and 'we'.

Third person omniscient: this is where the invented character takes no part in the story but instead, hovers over all of the characters and events, like a god. They know everything that happens to all of the characters, as well as all of their thoughts and feelings. They use the personal pronouns 'he', 'she', 'him', 'her', 'they' and 'them'.

Third person focalised: this is similar to third person omniscient *and* first person. Rather than knowing everything and everyone, this narrative voice is attached to a single character. As with first person, this narrator knows the actions, thoughts and feelings of only one particular character, and insight into other people only comes second-hand. However, they are not actually inside that character, but standing outside and observing. They use the same personal pronouns as third person omniscient.

Second person: this is much rarer than the other narrative perspectives, but can be surprisingly effective for certain types of stories. This is where the story is related as though the readers themselves had performed the actions, lived through the events, felt the emotions, and thought the thoughts of the character being described. This narrator uses the personal pronoun 'you'.

Choosing a Perspective

With these various options, choosing which perspective to use will depend on how you want to tell the story.

Using the first person perspective allows you to

tell the story from the inside. You can get extremely close to the action, and relate the events as though you were the protagonist and were telling it directly to the reader. This is an intimate form, but it does have the restriction that you cannot step outside of your character to know what is happening offstage, or in another character's mind.

Third person focalised works in a similar way, though there is an extra distance which gives you more leeway in what you tell. It also allows you to describe your character and their actions from outside, which is useful if they are unsympathetic, unlikely to be a useful narrator, or even if they are going to die before the end of the story.

Third person omniscient give you most distance from your protagonists. It is useful if you need to tell the story of more than one main character, and allows you to swap between them with ease. It also allows you to tell larger, more sprawling stories. It does lack focus and intimacy, however, so you need to decide if the trade is worth it.

Which perspective you chose to use will depend on the story you are telling, and how you want to tell it. However, one thing worth noting about narrative perspective is that if a story is not working, changing the person in which you are writing it can often change the dynamic and rescue the story.

DO IT NOW!

Chose a moment from your last week, something which you think might be interesting to write about. Now, write this scene in the **first person**, remembering what you felt and what you thought at the time, detailing the events that happened to you, and the outcome.

Once you have completed that, it's time to write it again.

Try it once in the **third person** – whether omniscient or focalised is up to you, chose based on what the story requires.

Then try it in the **second person**, so that the events happened to someone else who you address as 'you'.

When finished, read them over and see which works best, which you were most comfortable with, and which fits the story better.

The Implied Reader

When you write, unless you are writing a letter or an email to a specific recipient, you do not know who will be reading your work. As such, the piece you write will make assumptions about the reader of the work. On top of this, the narrator themselves might be addressing their tale to a specific, usually fictional, person

In order to take this into account, when writing, consider who is being addressed by the narrator. If it is not a specific person to whom the narrator is relating the story, then think about who is likely to pick up and read your story. Ask yourself the question 'Who is my audience?'

Bearing this in mind will affect how you write the story. If you are writing a story in a particular genre, then your audience will presumably be the kind of people who read those kinds of stories. As such, you can assume they have a certain basic knowledge of how things work in those genres, so you don't need to explain what you are doing.

If, however, you are writing for a more general audience, you might need to add a little more detail to stop them from becoming lost.

In doing this, your story will generate an 'implied reader', i.e.: the ideal person that your story is aimed at. Don't worry about the 'actual reader' as readers are flexible and will alter their assumptions of the story based on what you imply.

This isn't always a crucial consideration, but it is always worth bearing in mind in order to get your tone and perspective right.

Tenses

Another way of changing the perspective of a story, is to think about the point in time at which the story is being narrated, relative to the actual events.

There are two main ways:

- **Past Tense**: This is the more traditional storytelling mode. The narrator is telling the story after the events have occurred: 'He walked down the street and bumped into a lamppost.'

  This tense can usually be used in two different ways. In the first, the narrator is telling the story from after the whole thing has finished. They are looking back on all of the events and relating them with knowledge of how they will all turn out. Alternatively, although being told in the past tense, the narrator can be relating the story from a time point just after each event has been completed. In this version, they do not know what will happen next, or how the story will turn out in the end.

- **Present Tense**: This is used to give immediacy to a story. The narrator is relating the events as they occur, in the moment: 'He walks down the street and bumps into a lamppost.'

  This tense allows for the story to unfurl with no suggestion that the narrator knows the future events, or the ending. As a less traditional mode, however, it can be a little wearing in longer pieces, but it is often perfect for flash-fictions.

- **Other Tenses**: Other tenses do exist, and can be used for storytelling, but they tend to be less common, or used in conjunction with other tenses. These include the **Past Progressive** ('He was walking down the street and bumping into a lamppost.'); the **Past Perfect** ('He had been walking down the street and he had bumped into a lamppost.'); the **Future**

('He will walk down the street and will bump into a lamppost.')

From these examples, you can probably see how these other tenses can combine with the two main storytelling modes above, but they are less-often used on their own to narrate stories. They could, however, be used in that way in more experimental pieces (see below for more on experimentation.)

Again, as with your choice of narrator, your choice of tense will determine the level of immediacy in your story, and will be determined by how you want the story to be told, and to be read.

DO IT NOW!

Take your favourite of the stories written in the exercise above. Is it written in the past or present tense?

Whichever tense you have written it in, now rewrite it in the other (ie: change past to present, or present to past.) Do not simply change the tense in the original, but rewrite it completely in the new tense. Pay attention to how this changed storytelling mode can give you new possibilities and new limits which differ from the other.

Structure

We learn from an early age that stories are made up of three parts, a beginning, a middle, and an ending, and this is quite literally true. Every story will have words which start it, words which end it, and the bit in the middle. Likewise, a plot will have the first events, the middle events, and the last events.

However, one of the joys of writing is that while the story itself will always be made up of words in a particular order, the events of the plot do not have to be told in this order.

One particular technique – often used in film and TV – goes by the Latin term: *in media res*. This translates as 'in the midst of things' and refers to stories which start either in the middle of the plot, or towards the end, when many things have already happened. This is a useful technique because it means you can start with the most exciting part of the plot, grabbing the reader's attention. It also means that you can start writing without filling in any backstory, forcing the reader to read on so they can understand the context in which these events are happening.

In doing this, it is usually necessary to fill in the prior events as you go along – either by stopping the forward narrative and cutting back to the beginning, or by filling in the past details, piece by piece, as the rest of the story unfolds.

This technique is especially useful in flash-fiction as it fits nicely with the injunction often given to scriptwriters, but also applicable in flash-fiction* to 'get in late, get out early'. Or, in other words, to make sure you include only the important events, and let the rest be implied – implication being one of the key points of our understanding of flash-fictions.

Of course, you can still tell a story in the traditional beginning-middle-end way, but ensure that all parts are equally necessary for the story, and that you are going to hold your reader's attention all the way through.

Experimentation

The concepts discussed in this chapter show the most common ways of using perspective, tense and structure. However, these elements – perhaps more than the others which make up the writing of flash-fictions – give us the greatest scope for experimentation.

---

*And, I would argue, all writing...

Flash-fictions are a perfect form for experimental writing, as new techniques can be tried in a small, easily-controlled fashion, and are not so extended that you will entirely lose the reader.

There are more ways of experimenting with a piece of writing than I can fit here. They could take up a whole book by themselves, and it would still not be exhaustive (plus, the nature of experimentation means that there are ways I haven't even dreamed up yet, so I couldn't include them if I wanted to). However, here are some ways in which these techniques can be used to write flash-fictions in an experimental way:

- **Perspective**: The most obvious way is to mix them up and fragment the story into paragraphs in first person and others in third person. Or you could use multiple, different first person/third person focalised perspectives in different paragraphs/sections.

  Second person, as it is so little used, is quite an experimental perspective by itself, so is often a way in which new ways of storytelling are found.

  Stream-of-consciousness is a form of first

person narrative in which an attempt is made to represent the actual thoughts of the narrator, complete with random tangents, incomplete and overlapping thoughts, and often with fragmented grammar and a lack of punctuation.

- **Tenses:** As mentioned above, there are two standard storytelling tenses. Using anything other, or mixing up the traditional forms, perhaps in different paragraphs/sections will allow for experimentation. The future tense, especially, is ripe for experimental techniques, as it constitutes a prophecy rather than an existing story being related. It also allows for use of the conditional (could) and subjunctive (should) to suggest possibilities and choices.

- **Structure**: Any deviation from the standard 'Beginning-middle-end' structure, allows for experimentation. Mixing up the events and telling them in a seemingly random order is one way. Another might be to start and the end and work back to the beginning.

Of course, all of these possibilities for experimentation do not need to exist in isolation. The real fun emerges when you start to mix them up. Consider a second person story told in the future tense, where the narrator is telling the reader 'You will do this... You could do that...'

Or you can have a fragmented structure in which different parts of the story are told by different first person narrators, in different tenses.

One other way of experimenting, which wasn't mentioned above as it asks you to tell the story in a non-standard way, is to write something which is no longer a straightforward flash-fiction:

- **Form**: This is where you are still telling the events of a plot, but you appropriate a different form or writing. So, you might tell the story through TV listings. Or through the appointments in a diary. Or through an internet search history. Or as a footnote to an essay. Or in a shopping list. The possibilities here are truly endless, and can lead to some fascinating and interesting stories.

Once you start to play with the various methods of experimentation, it can be quite hard to stop, and you will always find new ways to write new stories. One note, however: make sure that the techniques and form that you chose are right for the story you want to tell. Communicating the story to the reader should be your primary intent. The experimentation should enhance how you tell it and also the enjoyment for the reader, but experimentation for its own sake loses its effectiveness.

EXERCISE

You are going to write a story in which three old friends from school meet up at a reunion. There is a big secret which is going to be revealed. Write the story in three sections — each one told in the first person by a different character. Consider the tense, and the ordering of events. At what point are you going to reveal the secret?

8. Reflection

In which we take a look back, a look around, and think about what exactly it is we're doing when we write flash-fictions.

Periodically, it's worth stepping back from actually doing the writing to think about what you're doing and how you are doing it. This reflection allows you to understand what you have learned – either from successes or failures – and what you can take forward into your writing.

Personally, I use a blog for this, and every so often I write about what I've learned, realised, worked out etc. It's a great way of marshalling thoughts. A notebook would work just as well, however. It's up to you how you reflect, what's important is that you do.

No work that you do, in flash-writing or anywhere else for that matter, is ever wasted, whether it is the simpler 'Do it Now!' or 'Toolbox' exercises, writing hooks, gathering prompts, or writing half a story which you abandon when it doesn't quite work out.

Now, I said 'anywhere else', but I do think that flash-fiction is a special case. Because the stories are so short and are, in many ways, simply a 'moment' of a larger story, they can often generate new prompts even from within a story that fails to work.

Reflecting on what you have done gives you a way to capture these ideas, tangents and fragments before they disappear, and hopefully helps you complete more of your stories, and avoid the pitfalls which might lead to a story not working out.

DO IT NOW!

It's time for you to think about what you have learned from reading this book and undertaking the various exercises.

Now, this is not a question of simply looking back over the content of the chapters. No. This is about what you have learned. It may be that some of what I have said is stuff you already knew. Some of it might not have been useful to you. And some of what you have learned might have come from your own thinking when you were writing, or out walking, or doing the dishes.

So, sit down and write a decent sized paragraph about what sticks in your head about flash-fiction. What have you learned? What are you going to bear in mind when writing? What are you going to avoid doing? Do you feel you understand flash better? Do you think your writing has changed?

That exercise was reflection aimed specifically at the activity of reading this book, but is something you should do regularly with regard to your writing. If you have a sudden insight into how something works, or how you prefer to write, then capture it in a paragraph of re-flection. Even if the insight has not arrived, set aside a time each day/week/month (whatever suits you best) to reflect on what you have done since your last reflection, and what you plan to do next. By capturing this experience in words, you give yourself something you can look back over, and see your progress. It also forces you to consider what you are doing and try to make sense of it. And by having it in writing it means that these thoughts will not be lost to the ether.

DO IT NOW! and TOOLBOX

Yes, I've incorporated these two together again. This is something you need to do before you read on, but it's also something you need to keep doing if you want to really get the hang of flash-fiction and keep improving. This is about reading as a writer.

So, go and find some flash-fictions. There are lots of places to find them simply through searching for 'flash-fiction' (with or without the hyphen) on the internet. Or you can search for anthologies, magazines, and there are a number of online magazines which print flash-fictions. If you're stuck, FlashFlood from National Flash-Fiction Day has hundreds at http://flashfloodjournal.blogspot.co.uk/

Find as many different writers as you can, as many different genres as you can, as many different styles as... you get the point. Lots of different stories.

To start with, just read. Allow yourself to decide which ones you like and which ones you don't. Think about why you might have these preferences. Oh and keep track of what you're reading as you might want to come back later.

Then, when you have finished reading, go and

do something else for a while. Take a break from them, let them seep into your head.

Done that? Good.

Now, the next step is to go back and find three of them that stayed with you. Three that made an impression, that you particularly liked (or didn't like). Write a paragraph or so for each of these, trying to explain what you think the story is doing. What effects has the author used? How have they told the story? What is it in the telling of the story that appealed (or didn't appeal)?

Try to put yourself in the mind of the writer and see what decisions they took in their creation. Bear in mind that the author's decisions may not have been conscious ones, but I think you will be able to see what they were nonetheless.

As you go through, think about the things that have been covered in this book. If the prompt is mentioned, look at how they have gone from prompt to story. Have they used any sensory input – things seen, heard, felt, smelt or tasted? Is there a hook? Does it work? How is character portrayed? What is the plot? Is there a larger theme beyond the basic plot? How is the story structured? Is there dialogue? If so, what purpose does it serve?

Try your best to take the story apart and see how it works.

Yes, I know this is similar to Literary Criticism in a way, and is almost like writing an essay, but it's an important task. And it differs from Lit Crit in that you are looking at it from a writer's perspective. In Lit Crit we would focus on theme, context, political and cultural influences. In this case we are looking much more at the 'nuts and bolts': we want to know how the thing is constructed, how it fits together, what powers it and makes it move.

This is, as I said, a TOOLBOX exercise as well as a DO IT NOW! It is something you should aim to do regularly when you come across a story that you think works well. Try to find out for yourself how it achieves what it does, and then you can start to apply those features to your own writing.

Flash-Fiction vs Short Story

Now, I must make a confession at this point. A large amount of what has been covered in this book are the basic tools not just for flash-fiction writing, but for short story writing in general. All short stories hopefully deal with hooks and plot, characters and dialogue, descriptions which rely on the five senses, etc. Hopefully I have also tied these features back to their specific use in flash-fictions, but they are certainly things you could use for writing longer pieces with a greater level of forward planning.

So, this seems like a good time to revisit our thoughts on flash-fictions as something different from short stories.

First, there is length. If you go back to the many definitions of flash-fictions that we looked at in Chapter 1, the main idea behind all of them is that this something which is generally shorter than your average short story. This brings a burden of its own in terms of writing.

Flash-fictions need to be really short. Some of this can be achieved through editing – which we will look at more in the last chapter – but it also needs to be embedded in the idea of the piece from the first sentence you write. What does this mean? Well, it means cutting to the chase. We don't have time to tell a huge amount of backstory so we have to start at the crucial point in the action. If you find your flash-fiction is too long, you need to ask if you have started too early on in the plot. Can you start later?

This sudden jump into narrative is going to

make your opening line all the more important – hence the examination of hooks – and also means that you are going to have to make your reader do a lot of work. To do this you need to imply a lot of information that your reader will bring with them – most commonly cultural references in terms of names, places, jobs, language etc.

You will also need to ensure that the information you give is specific and detailed and occurs in as few words as possible. There is no space for rambling generalities, nor for repetition of ideas. Every word has to count.

The next thing is to think about that aspect that makes the flash-fiction much more similar to poetry than the short story. That is the idea of theme. Novels, films, plays, short stories, flash-fictions and poems all have themes. These may also be termed 'morals' as in, 'the moral of the story is…'

In a novel, film and play, there will be many different themes. In a short story there will often be more than one. In a flash-fiction, as is often the case in poetry, there is generally only one. There just isn't the space for more. And to try and include too many would dilute the message of any individual theme. So something that flash-fiction is good for is conveying a single theme through the narration of an event.

When asked, I have often used the analogy that a flash-fiction is like a single malt whisky – as opposed to the pints of beer or glasses of wine which are novels and short stories – in that it conveys all its complexity in a single sip. It also manages to have a great impact with that one taste which can leave your audience gasping. That doesn't mean it needs to be violent or shocking, simply that the concept you are conveying is done so in such a concentrated, distilled way that you audience feels they have taken in a huge amount of information very, very quickly.

So, basically, to sum it all up, you need to use all the same tools as for a short story, but you need to boil it down to a single strand which you transmit to your reader quickly and cleanly and with all the power you can muster.

EXERCISE

What else could you do at this point but write some flash-fictions?

These should be extra short, so you have a word limit of 200 words. Try to write at least three, but more if you want to.

I am not going to give you any prompts – you know how to find those for yourselves now. I

93

am not going to stipulate whether you use character or plot, senses or dialogue. I want you to use all of them as you need to.

I am only going to make two rules:

1. You should attempt to write three *different* stories in, if possible, a single sitting. So, different styles, different genres, different perspectives, different themes. The exact 'difference' is up to you, but they should be distinct from one another.

2. Attempt to write at least one one story in a style/genre/perspective/etc. that you are uncomfortable writing in. So, if you don't like science-fiction, write that. If you don't like romance, write that. If you don't like really wordy Victorian-style writing, write that. If you don't like stories written from a child's perspective, write that. You get the point. Move out of your comfort zone and do something that you would not normally do. It's only by doing this that we expand our abilities.

9. Editing, Rewriting and Publication

*In which we break out
the polish and the dusters and
buff our stories to a perfect shine.*

Over the course of this book we have looked at what flash-fiction is, how to get ideas to write about, how to actually write the stories, and how to make them different, interesting and engaging. This chapter looks at what to do with the stories once you've written them as, sadly, typing the final full stop is not actually the end.

Editing

When you finish writing a flash – a mere few hundred words banged out in a handful of minutes – my advice is to walk away from it for a while. You've done the job, give yourself a rest. If you smoke, have a cigarette and think about other things. If you like coffee, go and make yourself one. If you're in the mood, play a couple of games of solitaire or minesweeper. Whatever you do – and you might have spotted the theme in these suggestions – only make the break a few minutes. You need to come down from wherever it is you go when you write, but I think you shouldn't go too far. You should still be in shouting distance of that place.

With a novel, I would advise making that break about three months. With a short story, about three weeks. But with a flash, I reckon 10-20 minutes is enough.

Now, when you come back to your piece, the first thing to do is read it. When I do that I'm often surprised. I don't remember writing some bits, and the whole thing looks different than I remember. That's good. It shows that you have come back to yourself from your writing place. Now you can edit.

Editing is not just about clearing up typos – it certainly is that, but not just that – it's about taking a piece and moulding it into a single whole. So, think about the piece. Think about the theme, the character, the setting, the plot, get them clear in your head, then go through and tweak the language. Does the voice of the narrator slip at any point? Does colloquial become formal or vice versa? Do the sentences stumble under the weight of an awkward word or construction? Can you replace a descriptive word with another which better carries your theme throughout the piece? Can you hold back the revelation a little bit longer? Do you repeat an idea? Do you carry on past the point where the story ends? Can you emphasise anything crucial?

In 1000 words – which is the absolute maximum you should be looking at – it is possible to consider the role that every word is playing and decide whether it is the best word, or even if it is necessary at all.

You can even, if you are very ruthless, spot that two different events in the story are really doing the same thing. If they are, get rid of one of them. Cut and edit, craft and mould, and remember that in as short a piece as a flash-fiction, each word will have much more impact.

One thing I like to do is to think of the theme, then think of words associated with that theme, and then try to use a number of them through-out the piece but in places where they are not necessarily obvious. That way, the accumulation of language is telling your story, rather than you having to play out the plot.

An example: if I want to tell a story about bereavement, I could include references to something (a pen, maybe) being 'lost', a wall having a 'hole' in it, the sky going 'dark', the bark of a tree being 'black' etc. I could tell the story of someone getting ready to leave the house and go for a walk, but with the accumulation of those words, the ideas of loss and bereavement would come through.

So, as you are probably realising, this is at least as big a job as the writing in the first place, and possibly even bigger. Don't let this worry you. If you let yourself, you can enjoy the editing, because as a story comes together, it's very satisfying. The other thing to realise is that this is a job which won't always take as long. As you write more flash-fictions (and trust me, I know that of which I speak!) you will find that you start incorporating the elements of editing into your writing. You don't plan to, but as you improve you will find that your consistency and sense of rhythm improve, that you start to sense your theme as you write and so the language follows.*

---

* If you want to investigate the world of editing in greater detail – and not just flashes, but longer stories and novels – see the other book in this series: *The Whole World in an Edit: How to Edit, Redraft and Rewrite.*

DO IT NOW!

Take a story that you wrote in one of the earlier exercises and edit it. Bear in mind everything you have learned, and everything listed above, and have a really good go at it. You might find you really hack at it, that's fine. Just knock it into what you consider to be a good shape.

When you have done that, write a small piece of reflection on the process. What did you change? Why did you change it? How have you improved the story? What lessons can you carry forward from the process.

What's next?

One of the hardest things for many writers is actually forcing themselves to do the writing. There is always another Facebook post to make, another funny cat to laugh at, another cup of tea to make, another oven to clean, another whatever. So, my advice is to find a time of day when you can consistently have a bit of space. If you haven't got one already, get up earlier or go to bed later to make it, but find that space. Even if it's just 10 minutes, that's enough. And that is your writing time. Whatever else is happening, that is the time to shut out the world and do your thing. If you make it the same time every day (and yes, I do mean *every* day) you will soon find that if you miss one you feel all strange…

So, that's one good way to make yourself write. I also find the threat of mass public humiliation works. I have undertaken projects to blog a new flash-fiction every day for a year, to write flash-fictions live on stage, and to write a full collection every month for a year (currently in progress at the time of writing). I'm sure I would have given up on many of these a long time before they were finished if it wasn't for all the people watching me do it.

Now, you don't have to be as extreme as me, but if you can find a writing partner, and egg each other on, that works just as well. You don't need a full audience, one person who will say 'oi! Where's today's story, then?' is enough.

Or, failing all of that, you can use good old fashioned will-power and motivation.

There may come days, however, when you think 'What's the point? I'll never be JK Rowling or Dickens or (fill in name of favourite author here).' No, chances are you won't. But if that's why you're writing, you should probably not be doing it. I write because I have to, because it makes sense of the world for me, and, honestly, because when a story goes well it is the best feeling I have ever had with my clothes on. I love to write, but for some reason I also resist doing it. So I have to find a way to make myself do it, and then all is well.

Publication

Another reason for writing is for publication. And I think that is something all writers should be thinking about. I don't mean that overnight you are going to get a mega book deal (though if you do, remember me…) but that there are lots of places out there, in paper and online, that are looking for flash-fictions. And the feeling of getting something accepted, even for a website, is second only to writing in the first place.

Yes, when you start sending things out you might be rejected, but that happens to everyone. If I send out ten pieces, I expect anywhere between half and all of them to come back saying 'no thanks'. Do I stop? Nope, I keep submitting. And, when I do get one of the rare acceptances, I don't stop then, either. I keep submitting. It's the only way.

A quick search of the internet will reveal many

places which publish flash-fiction in print as well as on the web.

And, if you start thinking about publications, then that gives you another reason to keep writing. After my year of projects, I am now in the position of having about 200 stories in my story bank, and I regularly send a batch out into the world. I try my best to fit the story to the publication. Many come back, but some get accepted. And with each one that finds a home I realise that I am getting better at this thing called 'being a writer'.

So, what am I saying? Well, find a way to keep writing. Once you have written, edit, edit, edit, and then send them out into the world and let other people enjoy what you have done. At the end of the day, writing is about communication, and if you don't let others read it, you're only talking to yourself.

EXERCISE

Let's go back to the beginning. I want you to revisit the senses exercise. But this time, I want you to expand each one. Make each into a little story. No more than 150 words for each one, but take some element of the sensory world around you and fictionalise it. Add character, add setting, add dialogue or whatever you want. But you should write 5 little stories which use the things you can sense around you as prompts.

Sample Stories

*In which you can read some of
my own flash-fictions and see
how some of the ideas turn into stories.*

Prompt-based flash-fiction

This story was written when I was using the names of colours on a paint chart as prompts. Other titles included: 'Raspberry Diva', 'Mud Hut' and 'Lost Lake'. The names of things like paints and nail varnishes make for surprisingly useful prompts.

Spring Blush

Winter had departed early and the woods were filled with crocuses and bluebells. The stalks of daffodils poked up here and there but had yet to sound their fanfare. The day was warm, even though it was not quite March, and Jack had dug his light-summer jacket out from the wardrobe.

He stepped between the flowers, not wanting to disturb them and Jill followed after him.

Since they had met their names had become a standing joke for friends and family alike. When they moved in together they had been overwhelmed with buckets, vinegar and brown paper. At first it had annoyed Jack, but now he was used to it. And it didn't matter what she was called, he was in love with this woman and nothing could put him off.

The thin sunshine broke through the sparse canopy and warmed them as they walked. Jack started to feel warm, even in such a thin jacket, but he kept it zipped up.

Finally they broke from the trees and into a clearing. It had obviously once been part of a path, the rest of which had been swallowed up. There was a bench to one side and then a small bridge over a stream.

They walked up onto the bridge and looked down into the water, the reflection of blue sky sparkling back at them.

Jill looked around and gave a happy sigh. "This is one of the most beautiful places, Jack. Thank you for bringing me here."

He nodded and kissed her lightly on the lips, then stepped back and started to unzip his jacket. He opened his mouth to speak, but Jill was looking away across the clearing and spoke before he could.

"Did you know it's been four years since we met?" She turned back and looked at him. He nodded. She gave a little laugh. "Of course, in a way, it's only our first anniversary. And that means this is the perfect time to do this."

She sank down onto one knee in the middle of the bridge and pulled a small box from her bag. She opened it to reveal a plain silver band.

"Jack, it's the twenty-ninth of February. I love you. I want to be with you forever. Will you marry me?"

Jack stood, looking down at her, a strange half-smile on his face, and said nothing.

Jill held the ring up a little higher, her own smile slipping a little. "Jack?"

He unzipped his jacket the rest of the way and reached into the inside pocket and pulled out a small black box. He opened it to reveal a gold ring with a single clear diamond set into it. He gave a shrug, a grin bursting on his face. "I will if you will."

Character-based flash-fiction

This story was prompted by an event in a newspaper (I think you'll find it quite easy to spot what it was) however, that prompt brought this character to mind. There is not a lot of plot in this piece, and most of what there is happens off page. It is, instead, a piece about a character at a difficult point in his life, and the accompanying emotions.

Rain Stops Play

Harry sat and watched the match, all the while wondering at what point it would be called off. The clouds had been thickening since lunchtime, the day growing ever darker as it progressed. It was a tough call as to whether it would be the arrival of rain or the lack of light which would cancel the match, but either way it seemed inevitable.

He had always enjoyed going to the cricket, whatever the weather. Margaret had complained that she was a cricket widow as, during the summer months, he would spend his weekends in the local grounds: large and small, county and international. He just loved the game. The white of the kit against the green of the grass, the careful defensive shots and the wild swings for victory, the regimented timing of 6 balls an over before changing ends, and a pause for tea. There was an order and a tradition to it which suited Harry.

Margaret had done the teas, sometimes, when the cricket came to their village, but apart from that she had taken no part in his hobby. And that was okay with Harry. He had his cricket and she had her garden.

He thought of the dead and dying roses waiting at home, of the weed-strewn borders and the lank yellow grass.

He still enjoyed the cricket but it just wasn't the same now. It didn't have that feeling of being a secret pleasure when he was alone all the time.

A call came from the field. Play was being abandoned for bad light.

Harry looked at his watch. It was five o'clock. Little chance they would resume today, but along with a handful of others he held his seat, while most of the spectators took this as their cue to leave.

A few minutes later, it started to rain, and the remaining die-hards gathered their belongings and made their way from the stands.

Harry stayed where he was and let the rain fall.

A flash-fiction of hooks and questions

The prompt for this story was a character created in a poem by another writer with whom I was collaborating. The character was a mostly silent man: one of a band of cowboys. Much of this is absent from my finished story which asks many more questions than it answers, yet uses this to create character and emotion and a story which, I hope, lingers in the mind after reading.

Tom

They don't ask. I can see the question in their eyes, but they don't ask it. It's not 'cause they don't want to know. I can see it burning them up. It's 'cause they're afraid I might answer.

Every morning, when I wake, I can feel the tension. A night's sleep feels like I've run twenty miles in the midday sun.

Every morning, when I wake, I can see the question riding their eyes, waiting to be asked.

Every morning, when I wake, I'm simply thankful that I'm no longer asleep.

I sometimes think the Kid will ask. He's new to this game and to the bigger game of life. But even he's learned enough not to ask.

Any man here has seen more than they

wanted to, more than they can escape. They don't want to shoulder anyone else's burdens. That's not how it goes on the trail.

I cry in my sleep, I know that. I cry in my dreams too, and the way it wracks my body carries on into my waking. My face is never wet, but my eyes burn with the unshed tears.

Why am I crying? That's what they want to know. That's what they always want to know. That's the question which will never be asked, and never be answered, and in the end will force them to drive me away. It's happened before and it'll happen again.

It's a question which grows every time it's left unasked, and in time it'll be too much for them. Their imaginings will make it bigger and badder 'til they can't bear to look at me.

I guess some of them think they should ask it because whatever it is couldn't be worse than what they have in their heads. But they still don't ask.

Every morning, when I wake, I'm thankful to escape my dreams, but I can never escape my memories. And every morning, when I wake, I'm sad to find I've woken up at all.

Plot-based flash-fiction

The idea for this story came during a workshop I was leading with students who had brought in pieces of music to act as prompts. I have no record of the song, or the band, but I know that the image of this man running through a collapsing space-station came to me and wouldn't leave. While there are other elements in this piece, it is the tension of the plot which drives it.

Shock Corridor

"This area is non-operational!" came the calm voice over the speaker.

Injit was not calm. He was running for his life.

Behind him the bulkhead door shot closed with a blast of air that wanted to knock him from his feet. He rode it, letting it carry him, and then planted his feet and kept going.

A crash and roar rocked the station as the section behind him crumpled and surrendered to the vacuum. Fuel cells detonated and tremors rocked the floor under Injit. He staggered and bounced against the wall, but he kept his feet and carried on.

There had been no warning. He didn't know

what had happened. A momentary hole in the shield? A micro-meteor just too large and travelling just too fast to be stopped? It didn't matter now. The imperative was to get away from the rolling collapse and get safe.

Gravity shifted under him and the floor became a slope. Injit dropped forward, his palms hitting the floorplates and skidding in blood. He ignored the pain and scrabbled forward, clawing his escape.

If he could reach the central hub, he could get to the shuttle and away. If the collapse stabilised he could return and begin repairs. If not, there was enough food, water and air in the shuttle to last him six weeks, long enough for help to come if he was lucky. But first he had to get there,

He clambered up and into the next section, sprawling over the raised threshold into the normal gravity on the far side. He dragged his feet over, pressed them to the ridge to boost himself upwards as the door flashed down just missing his heel. It was followed by the calm voice repeating its warning, barely audible over the crumple-crash of collapsing metal.

Injit's legs were starting to thrum in tune with the collapsing station, but he staggered on stiff legs and kept moving forward.

He was nearing the next section, just one away from the hub, when the lights started to flicker.

"This area is... This... non... This... Th-th-th-thhhrrrrrrrr..."

In the frantic strobing Injit slowed, and then an arc of electricity grounded to the plates in front of him with a bang. Injit pulled himself to a stop and watched as the corridor between him and the hub was lit by a lightning storm.

He looked back, but all was dark behind him. The sounds of creaking and crumpling were continuing. He couldn't go back. He couldn't stay here.

He faced forward, took a deep breath and thought of home.

Dialogue-based flash-fiction

I have developed a habit of writing some stories entirely in dialogue, with no narration at all. The first of these featured a pair of older, male characters called Bob and Jim. They keep returning as, it seems, they never run out of things to say. Here is their debut.

Cream Dust

- What's this colour then?
- Hang on… It says 'Cream Dust' on the tin.
- 'Cream Dust'? What kind of a name is that?
- What do you mean, it's creamy, isn't it?
- Yeah, sure, so why not just call it 'Cream'?
- Well, they have lots of creams, don't they?
- How can you have lots of creams. It's a colour, isn't it? It's *cream*.
- Ah, but they have shades.
- So do I. I wear 'em when it's sunny.
- Oh, ha ha. You know what I mean.
- I know, but 'Cream Dust'? I mean: 'dust'? Who wants to paint dust onto their walls. You paint the room to make it look better, cleaner, not dusty.
- I guess it's just cos it's kinda dusty in its feel. It's not like it's going to flake all over the place and leave the room looking a state.

- You should paint the room with Boddies.
- Ha, the cream of Manchester, eh?
- Yeah, till they bloody moved it.
- Bastards.
- You think they ever advertised Guinness as the cream of Dublin?
- Dunno. It was all toucans and being good for you.
- Are they?
- What?
- Toucans. Are they good for you?
- No, you silly bugger, Guinness. Guinness is good for you.
- Is it?
- No, not really. But that was the slogan.
- I thought it was about waiting.
- It was, but that was later.
- Had to wait for it, eh?
- Yeah. So, we going to paint this room, then?
- Could do, could do…
- Fancy a pint instead?
- Good call.

Experimental Flash-fictions

I must admit, I do a lot of this. I like to play with the form to see what it can do, and to find the ways in which a story can be told. So here, are two different approaches to two rather different stories.

Urban Obsession

He stood at the edge of town. Behind him was a garage selling petrol and pasties and dead flowers, a row of mostly-empty houses, and the road back to civilisation. In front of him were trees and grass and fields and the unknown.
He stood at the edge of town and examined the world, daring his feet to take another step.

She walked to the bus-stop in the fading light, her skin goose-bumping in the chill. Her clothes were tight and thin and hardly-there but would be too hot in the club. The wind tried to move her hair, but the mousse and spray held it tight.

On the bus she was aware of the glances. The olders looked at her with a mixture of horror, disgust and hidden lust. The youngers nodded to her, whether they knew her or not, and did nothing to disguise their lust or their envy.

As she stepped from the bus her foot sank into a puddle which left a line of brown over her white shoe. She bent down to wipe it with a finger and watched as a discarded McDonald's chip-carton scudded past.

It was going to be a cold night. He huddled into the doorway and pulled the torn blanket around him. Layers of clothing did little to keep out the chill, the fingers of the wind finding purchase in each tatter.

He could feel the damp stone underneath him. Last night he'd found some cardboard to separate him from the concrete, but it must have blown away in the day.

People walked past on the main road, heading to bars, to their work, to their homes. He watched them pass and tried to push himself deeper still into the doorway; tried to merge with the stone.

She trudged back from the hospital. Her father was worse. They said he might last the night, but didn't hold out much hope. They had offered her a bed, but what was the point? Would it make any difference if she stayed and watched him die?

She walked home to her children, past the

park. In the sick sodium light she noted the fresh graffiti. Daz loves Kat, does he?. She noted the glitter of broken bottles and the possibility of needles. She noted the weeds in the cracks in the rubber matting, fitted for children who never visited.

Two men walked towards her on the same pavement and she adjusted the keys in her hand. Just in case.

It was dark now, and the rain was starting again. He had watched the wind bend the trees and grass until they were swallowed in the lack of streetlights.

His feet had not moved, not taken him away. The wind had not lifted him into a land of Technicolor. Once more he had stood at the edge and looked out but been unable to move, to reach, to grasp.

He turned and walked back home, only stopping at the garage to buy a Twix.

The Bomb Only Lives While It's Falling

She didn't stop to think, she just leapt from her chair.
   That was what the witnesses said.

I can't believe she did it. It's just not like her.
   That was what her sister said.

She was very quiet, what with being wobbly on her pegs, you know? We barely saw her.
   That was what the neighbours said.

She was a mother of four, grandmother of six. Nothing more than an ageing housewife.
   That was what the papers said.

She came out of nowhere. She saved my life.
   That was what the security guard said.

Without her, he would have got away with a little over half a million.
   That was what the bank manager said.

She shouldn't've bin there. It should've bin the fucker with the cash.

That was what the gunman said.

She died from massive blood-loss due to gunshot trauma.

That was what the coroner said.

She was my wife, and she was always a hero to me.

That was what her husband said.

Now. Now is my time. At last, my time to act; my time to make a difference.

That was what she had thought.

Appendix

Hook Exercise answers

'It is a truth universally acknowledged, that a single man in possession of a good fortune, must be in want of a wife.' – **Pride and Prejudice by Jane Austen, 1813.**

'It was a bright cold day in April, and the clocks were striking thirteen.' – **1984 by George Orwell, 1949.**

'It was the best of times, it was the worst of times, it was the age of wisdom, it was the age of foolishness, it was the epoch of belief, it was the epoch of incredulity, it was the season of Light, it was the season of Darkness, it was the spring of hope, it was the winter of despair.' – **A Tale of Two Cities by Charles Dickens, 1859.**

'If you really want to hear about it, the first thing you'll probably want to know is where I was born, and what my lousy childhood was like, and how my parents were occupied and all before they had me, and all that David

Copperfield kind of crap, but I don't feel like going into it, if you want to know the truth.' – *The Catcher in the Rye* by **J.D. Salinger, 1951.**

'It was a pleasure to burn.' – *Fahrenheit 451* **by Ray Bradbury, 1953.**

'TRUE! nervous, very, very dreadfully nervous I had been and am; but why WILL you say that I am mad?' – **'The Tell-tale Heart' by Edgar Allen Poe, 1843**.

'------------**Mr Sherlock Holmes**, who was usually very late in the mornings, save upon those not infrequent occasions when he was up all night, was seated at the breakfast table.' – *The Hound of the Baskervilles* **by Arthur Conan Doyle, 1902.**

'Behavioral Science, the FBI section that deals with serial murder, is on the bottom floor of the Academy building at Quantico, half-buried in the earth.' – *The Silence of the Lambs* **by Thomas Harris, 1989.**

'There was no possibility of taking a walk that day.' – *Jane Eyre* **by Charlotte Brontë, 1847.**

'The sky above the port was the color of television, tuned to a dead channel.' –

Neuromancer by William Gibson, 1984.

'I had been making the rounds of the Sacrifice Poles the day we heard my brother had escaped.' – *The Wasp Factory* by Iain Banks, 1984.

Afterword

As I said in the introduction, this book has been adapted from an online course in flash-fiction which I have been running for the last few years with some success. It is just one of three courses I have run and the other two—covering life-writing and editing—will also be coming out as books shortly.

In the rest of my life I teach creative writing—mostly prose writing—at universities. I am also the founder and Director of National Flash-Fiction Day in the UK, and I am managing editor of my own small publishing house—Gumbo Press—which focuses on flash-fictions.

Beyond that, I am a flash-fiction writer with a number of collections out in the world should you feel like picking one up. At the time of writing I am engaged in a project to write and self-publish a new collection every month for a year, which is leading to some interesting research on the concept of combining flash-fictions into collections. That research will, with luck, form part of a second volume of *The*

Whole World in a Flash which will look at some advanced techniques and what can be done with flash-fictions beyond individual stories.

If you are interested in any of the things mentioned here, I have provided a series of links below which you might be interested in.

If you have enjoyed this book and found it useful, or if there is anything that you feel should be covered in the next volume, please feel free to get in touch to let me know.

Special thanks need to go out to Kath Kerr, Lorna Rutter and Gerald Hornsby, for their proof-reading skills, and to all the students who took the course, for helping me get it right.

Thanks for reading, and happy flashing!

Calum Kerr
Southampton
07/04/2014

Links:
www.calumkerr.co.uk
www.nationalflashfictionday.co.uk
www.gumbopress.co.uk

Flash-Fiction Collections available from Gumbo Press:

Threshold by David Hartley

Apocalypse by Calum Kerr

The Audacious Adventuress by Calum Kerr

The Grandmaster by Calum Kerr

Enough by Valerie O'Riordan

The Book of Small Changes by Tim Stevenson

Printed in Great Britain
by Amazon.co.uk, Ltd.,
Marston Gate.

DR CALUM KERR is a writer, editor, Teaching Fellow in Creative Writing at the University of Southampton's Winchester School of Art, and Director of the UK's National Flash Fiction Day. His work has appeared in a number of places—online and in print—and was featured on BBC Radio 4's *iPM* programme. He lives in Southampton with his wife, his stepson, two cats and a dog.

Other books by Calum Kerr

FLASH-FICTION COLLECTIONS

31

Braking Distance

Lost Property

2014 FLASH365 COLLECTIONS

1: *Apocalypse*

2. *The Audacious Adventuress*

3. *The Grandmaster*

NOVELS

Undead at Heart

NON-FICTION BOOKS

The World in an Edit (Coming soon)

The World in a Memoir (Coming soon)

York Notes Advanced: The Kite Runner

York Notes AS & A2: The Kite Runner